To Jess

Enjoy.

N. Sta

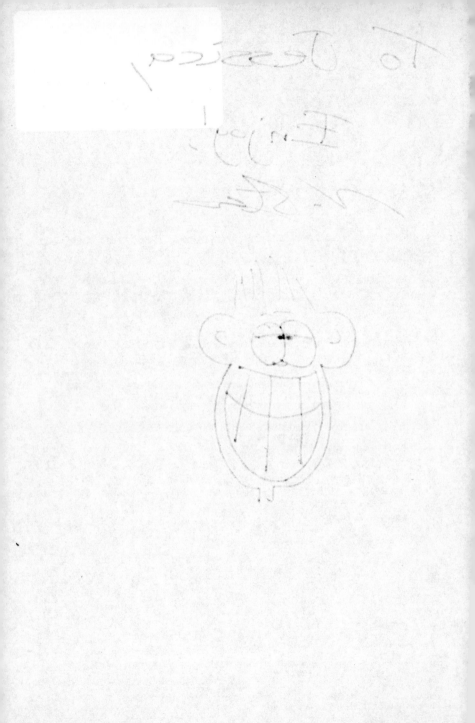

In Bits

In Bits is a collection of poems written by well-known poet Neil Stevens. This book is Neil's very first and in it he brings together a whole range of hugely enjoyable poems, covering all sorts of subject areas. So take the time to enjoy his work and find out how poetry can truly make you smile.

Neil Stevens is a trained teacher who lives in Kent. He set up his performance poetry business in 2003 and has performed in many Kent schools since then. He has also performed in a variety of well-known Kent based events and is now taking his performances countrywide. Find out more about Neil and his work at www.poeticpieces.com.

Dedicated to

Tianbi, Mingjian, Feng,
Bernadette, Len, Helen, Melanie
and all those who have believed (and still believe) in
Poetic Pieces.

In Bits!

Neil Stevens

Poetic Pieces Publishing

Published by
Poetic Pieces Publishing
83 Oswald Road,
Dover, Kent CT17 0JN,
England
www.poeticpieces.com
ISBN 0-9553518-0-4
ISBN 978-0-9553518-0-8

First edition 2006.

Printed and bound in China by
Nanjing Jiaoxin Technology Development Ltd, Nanjing

Contents

Some complete nonsense!

Some crazy characters!

Days in school!

Contents

General

All Join In!

In Bits!

When I woke up the other morning,
I really felt the pits,
And I couldn't pull myself together,
So I just had to stay in bits!

My feet went off to go shopping,
Looking around for some shoes,
Whilst my head stayed in bed watching telly,
Just catching up on all the news.

My legs went out into the garden,
And stretched themselves out on the grass,
And only my bottom went off to school,
And sat itself down in my class!

My stomach went out to go swimming,
And floated about in the pool,
My chest did its best to do something,
But ended up doing nothing at all!

My arms went on an adventure,
Down to the woods to climb trees,
Whilst my hands spent all day in the kitchen,
Cooking up pasta and cheese!

But when I woke up this morning,
No more was I under the weather,
So I had no problems finding all my bits,
And pulling myself together!

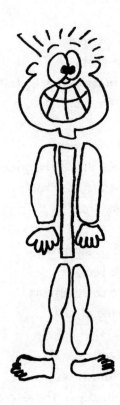

Have You Ever Seen?

Have you ever seen hamsters singing?
Or monkeys wearing shoes?
Or elephants swinging from the ceiling whilst reading out the news?

Have you ever seen lions painting?
Or frogs laughing lots and lots?
Or spiders in the kitchen using all the
pans and pots?

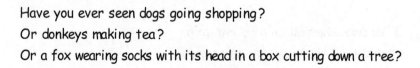

I've seen them all just the other night,
And boy did they give me a fright.

Have you ever seen hedgehogs dancing?
Or whales fight with swords?
Or cats wearing hats all swinging some
bats whilst riding on skateboards?

Have you ever seen dogs going shopping?
Or donkeys making tea?
Or a fox wearing socks with its head in a box cutting down a tree?

I've seen the lot just the other day,
And boy did they scare me away!

Have you ever seen rabbits in taxis?
Or moles on a mountain climb?

Or a giraffe in a bath wrapped up in a scarf whilst drinking a
glass of wine?

Have you ever seen swans knitting jumpers?
Or a horse ride a bike into town?
Or snakes baking cakes on a ship in some lakes whilst jumping
up and down?

I've seen them with my very own eyes,
And boy did they give me a surprise.

Have you ever seen fish going skiing?
Or chimpanzees chewing on chips?
Or goats' sailing boats up and down moats whilst doing
dramatic back flips?

Have you ever seen mice playing drum kits?
Or squirrels make castles with sand?
Or fleas up in trees doing handstands on bees whilst only using
one hand?

I've seen them all on a recent trip,
And boy did they make my heart skip!

The Island of Kuquagaloo

I've heard of a little island,
That's known as Kuquagaloo,
Its whereabouts are thereabouts,
And only known by a few,
So when you say that it exists,
Most say, "That's just not true."

On Kuquagaloo all the trees are yellow,
And all the grass is pink,
And better still on every hill,
There stands a kitchen sink,
With taps that speak and always ask you,
"Would you like a drink?"

There are talking elephants all coloured green,
Who bounce around on springs,
Whilst wearing crowns upon their heads,
For they love to look like kings,
And they hold long conversations,
About all sorts of silly things.

There are monkeys too all coloured blue,
Who all play in a band,
Playing funky little instruments,
On a beach of orange sand,
And there are mice who being nice,

Like to come and lend a hand.

In Kuquagaloo raindrops have legs,
And are all shaped like a square,
And when they hit the ground they all run around,
Running from here to there,
And when it rains it always smells,
Of apple, peach and pear!

There are insects on the island too,
Lots of different sorts,
And they're all very fit and very healthy,
For they play all kinds of sports,
Apart from all the ants,
Who just sit and write reports.

The fish in the sea off Kuquagaloo,
Believe that fish's rule,
So they just ride around on surfboards all day,
Trying to be cool,
And those fish you know,
They really don't do anything else at all.

There are cats on the island, some big and some small,
Who always jump at the chance,
To all get together whatever the weather,
For a jolly old song and a dance,
And they're all sorts of nationalities,
But most, they come from France.

On Kuquaglaoo, when night-time falls,
The stars come out and sing,
And the leaves on the trees swing around in a breeze,
For they all grow on pieces of string,
The rocks on the island love rolling about,
The birds on the island don't squawk they just shout,
The rivers and streams all flow uphill,
And nothing at all ever stands still.

The flowers on the island all smell of old cheese,
And there's nothing to eat there except carrots and peas,
In truth it's an incredibly strange place to go,
For Kuquagaloo is like nowhere we know.

But now you know of a little island,
That's known as Kuquagaloo,
And so when some they say, "It doesn't exist",
You say, "That's just not true!"

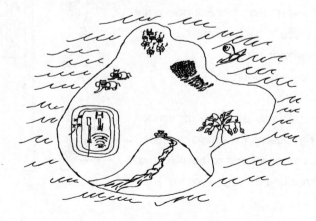

What Would You Do?

What would you do if one morning,
When you went down the stairs,
You found out that everyone else in the world,
Had turned into apples and pears!

Maybe you wouldn't be bothered,
Maybe you wouldn't feel glum,
Perhaps you'd just make a tasty fruit salad,
Out of your dad and your mum!

What would you do if one evening,
Whilst you were watching TV,
You heard that out of the zoo in the city,
A rhinoceros had broken free.

Maybe you wouldn't be panicked,
Maybe you wouldn't break into a sweat,
Perhaps you'd just catch it,
Tie it up to a tree,
And keep it as your pet!

What would you do if one afternoon,
Whilst you were mopping the floor,
A bunch of slimy and grimy old aliens,
Came knocking at your door!

Maybe you wouldn't feel flustered,
Maybe you wouldn't shriek,
Perhaps you'd just say,
"Come on in boys,
You can stay in my house for the week!"

What would you do if one day,
When you went to the beach for a swim,
You found that the sea had vanished,
So no longer could you jump in!

Maybe you wouldn't be worried,
Or have an anxiety attack,
Perhaps you'd just stroll,
All the way to America, say "Hello",
And then stroll back!

What would you do if so suddenly,
Dogs began to talk, saying,
"Don't worry about me this evening,
I'll just take myself out for a walk!"

Maybe it wouldn't surprise you,
And when you heard the news,
Perhaps you'd just say, "That's wonderful",
And give them some comfortable shoes!

What would you do if one weekend,
Whilst taking a snooze in a chair,

You woke up to discover,
That all of a sudden,
You had 35 metres of hair!

Maybe you wouldn't be fussed at all,
Maybe it'd just be your thing,
Perhaps you'd just have it tied to a pole,
And back and forth you'd swing!

Yes, if any of these things
Were to happen to you,
Just ask yourself,
What would you do?

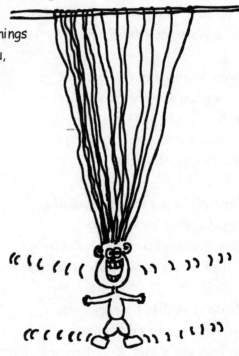

Something Nasty and Mean
In Our Washing Machine!

There once was something nasty and mean,
Lurking inside a washing machine,
I know this story and report it,
Because my mum and dad, they bought it.

It wasn't in our house for long,
Before I knew something was wrong,
For I saw and I was not mistaken,
That from the first wash a sock was taken!

I told my mum about my fear,
She said, "Oh don't be silly dear",
But I knew that it was there no doubt,
For two socks went in and only one came out!

I told my dad but he just said,
"Stop making things up in your head,
How on earth can something nasty and mean,
Be living inside a washing machine?"

I was not believed, so from that day,
From the washing machine I stayed away,
And still other socks went missing too,
And no one fussed but me I knew.

Then one morning oh so suddenly,
I woke to find my family,
Had all been put on 'red alert',
For now there was a missing shirt!

It was my dad's; it was his favourite,
He said, "Children yesterday I gave it,
To your mum to get it clean,
And she put it in our washing machine,
She filled it up and switched it on,
Some clothes came back but my shirt was gone,
So my children please be aware,
That something nasty and mean's in that machine right there!

We were all scared; my dad was vexed,
My mum said, "My whatever next,
We must deal with it I suppose,
Or soon we may lose all our clothes,
But we cannot do this on our own",
And so suddenly she grabbed the phone.

She called the police and the fire brigade,
And asked them both to come to our aid,
But when they heard of what we had,
They said, "Sorry madam that's just too bad,
That's too much of a risk to our health,
You'll have to deal with that one by yourself!"

So then my mum she called the army,
And they said, "Madam you must be barmy",
So instead she called on the marines,
Who said, "Maam just blow it to smithereens!"

So my dad said "Right" and then stood up,
Took it out the back and blew it up!
Now you can never be too careful it's true,
So that really was the best thing to do!

Now the point of this is although it may look nice,
When buying certain machines just think twice,
For you may take it home and be full of pride,
But something nasty and mean may lurk inside!

The Errabundyboo!

It may be small,
It may be big,
It may be bald and wear a wig,
And every morning it may dance a jig!
The Errabundyboo!

It may walk for days without stopping,
It may eat cheese with chocolate topping,
It may hate scrubbing but love mopping!
The Errabundyboo!

It may be thin,
It may be fat,
It may wear nothing but a hat,
And its favourite word may be 'this' or 'that'!
The Errabundyboo!

It may be fresh,
It may be smelly,
It may have short legs and one huge belly,
It may wear one green and one pink welly!
The Errabundyboo!

It may love standing on its head,
It may like cooking in a shed,
It may sleep standing up in bed!

The Errabundyboo!

And it may have 12 to 20 toes,
And may blow bubbles through its nose,
But how it looks, nobody knows!
The Errabundyboo!

Nuts About Nuts!

You know I'm nuts about nuts,
It simply must be reported,
That whether dry roasted, honey,
Or simply plain salted,
I'm crazy for peanut,
Pistachio or cashew,
Or whatever; I'm not fussy,
Any nut will do!

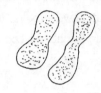

I eat nuts in the morning,
I eat nuts at night,
I eat nuts in the car,
I eat nuts on a flight,
I eat nuts at 1, at 2, or at 3,
Yes give me the choice,
And it's nuts for me!

Yes I'm nuts about nuts,
It simply must be said,
Everyday I have thoughts about nuts in my head,
I'm loopy and loony and crazy about them,
I think I'd go 'nuts',
If I was without them!

You know I'll say it again and again and again,
Yes I'm nuts about nuts,

I've got nuts on the brain,
Forget chocolate and sweets,
They don't make me smile,
I tell you my friends,
Just give me nuts by the pile!

Yes I'm nuts about nuts,
I'm a major nut fan,
I'm the nuttiest nut-loving nut in the land,
Just give me nuts I say,
And that will do,
And oh yes, I quite like crisps too!

All Mixed Up!

I like to piint some pactures,
For I like mainting pe,
And I love to munch on cruit fake,
With a tup of cea!

I like to flay some pootball,
And mance to dusic too,
And I love to cribble nisps,
Or see zonkeys at the moo!

I like to song aling to songs,
And dash on brums like hell,
And I love bleeping in my sed,
And ringing wells as bell!

I like to gig up the darden,
And wind some friggly worms,
But once I've finished I mash wyself,
To get gid of all the rerms!

I like to choff on scocolate,
And go pimming in the swool,
And I love to ho on golidays,
Because I think they're ceally rool!

I like to wun about the roods,
And tump on a jrampoline,
And I love to groll around in rass,
And turn my glothes all creen!

I like to bide my ricycle,
And stateboard down the skreet,
And I love to dalk around all way,
With frainers on my teet!

I like to rit down and selax,
And slay in the summer pun,
And I love to wix up all my mords,
Because I think it's foads of lun!

Sit 'On' Your Bottom!

Now only certain things are made for sitting on,
And that's the reason why we've got 'em',
So why on earth do they say in school,
"Ok now sit on your bottom."

For sit 'on' your bottom,
How can you do that?

For your bottom's not like an object,
That you can pick up and put down,
It's just a part of the body at the top of the legs,
(And that's where it can always be found)!

But just imagine if you could actually sit 'on' your bottom!

Then teachers would say ...

"Children don't leave your bottoms sticking out,
It's dangerous and you are all able,
To remember the rules; so when in school,
Tuck your bottoms in under the tables!"

Or ...

"Children please wait just a moment,
There are not enough bottoms for us all,

So please can you two boys right there,
Go and get some more bottoms from the hall!"

And imagine within your classroom,
There'd be one big bottom in its place,
And the teacher would say, "I want you all on the bottom please,
Everyone find a space!"

Or imagine if at the end of the day,
You had to stack all your bottoms away,
Yes stack up the bottoms one-by-one,
Bottoms on bottoms (or bums on bums)!

So there you have it!

In truth you must sit on something,
Like a chair or bench, the floor or a stool,
So when someone says, "Sit on your bottom please",
Just say, "I can't that's impossible!"

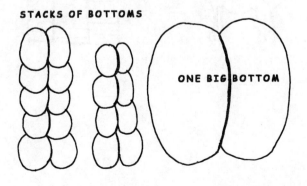

STACKS OF BOTTOMS

ONE BIG BOTTOM

The Difference Between Dogs and Sheds!

The difference between dogs and sheds,
Is that only dogs have heads and legs,
And let's not be silly; let's not pretend,
Whenever were sheds 'man's best friend'!

Mumbling Minnie

Little Minnie was sweet; she never fussed nor fumbled,
She never even tossed or tumbled,
And she certainly never grouched or grumbled,
But when Minnie spoke, she always mumbled!

She went, "Mmmrrmmmrrmmmrr."

Mum and Dad would say "What's that my dear?"
"You'll have to come closer, we didn't hear,
Whatever you said just wasn't clear",
But Minnie just went "Mmmrrmmmrrmmmrr."

She mumbled at one, or two, or three,
She mumbled at breakfast, lunch and tea,
And whether she was on land or at sea,
Minnie just went "Mmmrrmmmrrmmmrr."

She mumbled in a car, a train or a plane,
She mumbled in sunshine, in wind and in rain,
She mumbled in England, France and in Spain,
Mum and dad thought she would drive them insane.

They would say, "Minnie we don't want to kick up a fuss,
But we don't understand what you're saying to us,
This problem we really have to discuss",
But Minnie just went "Mmmrrmmmrrmmmrr."

She mumbled at home lots and lots,
And when she went shopping she mumbled in shops,
She mumbled whilst putting on her shoes and her socks,
All the time she just went "Mmmrrmmmrrmmmrr."

She mumbled all day, she mumbled all week,
Her mumbles were high, her mumbles were deep,
She even mumbled in her sleep!
She went "Zzzz, mmmrr, zzzz, mmmrr."

She mumbled when cold, she mumbled when warm,
She mumbled and mumbled from dusk till dawn,
She had mumbled since the day she was born,
Her whole life she just went "Mmmrrmmmrrmmmrr."

Then one morning Minnie heard dad say,
"You know Minnie I hope one day,
That all you mumbling goes away",
And Minnie turned around and said "Ok!"

Dad was quiet then suddenly he realised,
And leapt of his chair and widened his eyes,
And looked at Minnie so surprised,
And Minnie said "Ok."

"I don't believe it" he started to shout,
And waved his arms and jumped about,
And he ran to mum calling out,

"Minnie didn't mumble!"

And mum was just as happy as dad,
And they said to Minnie, "We're really glad,
It's not that mumbling is bad,
It's just hard to comprehend."

So from that day forward, to be sure she was heard,
Minnie decided to talk using words,
She said, "Who, why, what, where and when"
And she never went "Mmmrrmmmrrmmmrr" again!

Big Billy Bully and Enormous Ed!

Billy was a bully,
The biggest one in school,
He liked to fight with all his might,
He thought that it was cool!

If anyone argued with him,
Or didn't like what he said,
He would find them in the playground,
And bop them on the head!

He didn't have many friends,
Just a very small collection,
They use to hang around with Billy,
For their own protection.

And everybody else,
Knowing Billy was the boss,
All tried to be nice to him,
So they didn't make him cross.

So Billy was used to being King,
He wasn't scared at all,
No one could be bigger then Billy,
That was impossible.

But then one day when Billy came to school,
He heard a buzz in class,
There was nattering and chattering,
"What's going on?" he asked.

He found it all confusing,
So he stood and scratched his head,
Then teacher called out loud and clear,
"Everybody this is Ed."

"Ed is new to our class,
He starts with us today,
Be sure to make him welcome,
And let him come and play."

But the class just sat in silence,
Now Billy knew why there was a fuss,
He'd never seen anything like it before,
Ed was ENORMOUS!

It was totally unbelievable,
You couldn't help but be impressed,
Billy knew if he stood next to Ed,
He would only reach his chest!

For such a big event,
Billy really wasn't prepared,
And for the first time in his life,
Billy felt a little scared.

And quickly Ed made lots of friends,
As he was nice and liked to play,
Then one day when Billy went to bop someone,
Ed stood in the way!

Billy looked up at Ed's face,
"Get out the way" he asked,
Then he bashed and bopped and biffed Ed,
But Ed just stood and laughed!

Then the laughs got louder,
And the whole class laughed at Billy,
And he felt embarrassed, small and stupid,
And also very silly.

Then everybody said "Billy you're such a bully,
The biggest in the school,
But we don't like your bullying,
Because bullying isn't cool."

"Your bullying it hurts us,
And makes us feel sad,
No one really wants to be your friend,
You're a bully and you're bad!"

Then Enormous Ed looked down on Billy saying,
"Your bullying is a bore,
And I'm never going to let you,
Bully anyone anymore."

Billy looked around at everyone,
And saw lots of angry eyes,
And Billy felt so very bad,
That he apologised!

"I'm sorry" Billy said,
"I didn't mean to be so ghastly,
Or horrible and terrible,
And just so mean and nasty."

Then from that day on,
Billy didn't bully anyone again,
And now Billy, Ed and everyone,
Are all the best of friends!

Andrea Angel

Andrea was an angel,
So very, very sweet,
Her bedroom full of clothes and toys,
Was always very neat,
She never made a mess of things,
She always did her best at things,
She was the nicest little girl in the whole of her street!

Everyone that knew her,
Said they were really glad,
And if she ever went away,
They would all be very sad,
So imagine they could not believe their eyes,
And altogether were so surprised,
When one day Andrea woke up and went completely mad!

She threw her clothes out of the window,
And her toys all on the floor,
She stomped about the house,
Banging every single door,
She really didn't care at all,
She put her face in cereal,
No one had ever seen her do anything like that before!

She left her hair all messy,
Saying she thought that it was cool,

She ran off down the garden,
When it was time to go to school,
She wasn't gone for very long,
But came running back with nothing on!
Nobody had any idea of what to do with her at all.

She wouldn't sit still in the car,
And gave her sister a kick,
She jumped up and down on the seats so much,
She made herself get very sick,
Then she felt she needed more to munch,
So she took and ate her sister's lunch,
Then she looked her sister in the face and gave her one big lick!

In school when in assembly,
She sat and burped out loud,
When teacher said, "What do you say",
She said, "I'm very proud",
She paid no attention at all in class,
And answered nothing she was asked,
She just screamed and screeched all day
long making more noise than a crowd!

When her mother came to take her home,
Little Andrea shouted, "No",
And sat down on the carpet saying,
"I'm just not going to go",
And while she sat there in her place,
She took a pen and drew on her face,

"What's happened to Andrea?" teacher said,
And her mum said, "I don't know."

Then when going home mum decided,
They had to go to town,
And in every shop in which they stopped,
Andrea ran round and round,
She kept everybody busy,
Whilst she made herself get very dizzy,
Then she got her clothes all dirty by
rolling on the ground.

Back home Andrea wouldn't do homework,
She just sat and watched TV,
Then refused to move when her mother asked her to come and
eat her tea,
Then she jumped up and down on all the chairs,
And ran off laughing up the stairs,
Whatever had happened to Andrea was just a mystery.

Then suddenly Andrea stopped,
"I've had enough," she said,
"I've been mad for a whole day now and I want to go to bed,
Being mad is just too much trouble",
Then she gave her mum a cuddle,
And went upstairs very quietly to rest her weary head.

The next day when Andrea woke up,
She was very, very sweet,

And soon she was back to being the nicest girl in her whole street,
Now why she went mad once no one can explain,
They're just happy that Andrea's an angel again,
And they hope that all her madness is something she won't repeat!

Hungry Harry

Harry was always hungry,
He couldn't go a minute,
Without finding lots of food,
And sticking his face in it!
Whenever he went anywhere,
He carried on his back,
A bag full up with lovely grub,
So he could always have a snack.

And everyone would say,

"Harry don't you worry,
About making yourself sick?"
But Harry would say, "Not at all"
And just give his lips a lick!

He munched at 9 and crunched at 10,
He ate all morning until lunch and then,
He ate the biggest lunches you've ever seen,
And wouldn't stop until his plate was clean.
Yet after lunch he had room for more,
So he chewed at 3 and he chomped at 4,
Then gulped at 8 and gobbled at 9,
In fact Harry just ate all the time!

And everyone would say,

"Harry don't you worry,
About making yourself sick?"
But Harry would say, "Not at all"
And just give his lips a lick!

Harry was always happy too,
Never in a mood,
Just as long as he was surrounded,
By lots and lots of food,
And no matter how many times,
He ate breakfasts, dinners and lunches,
At any time of the day,
Harry always had the munchies.

And everyone would say,

"Harry don't you worry,
About making yourself sick?"
But Harry would say, "Not at all"
And just give his lips a lick!

And when it came to pie eating contests,
It came as no surprise,
That Harry always won the prizes,
Because he could eat up all the pies.
In fact any food he ever saw,
Harry would polish off,
It just seemed as if forever,

Harry would scoff and scoff and scoff!

And everyone would say,

"Harry don't you worry,
About making yourself sick?"
But Harry would say, "Not at all"
And just give his lips a lick!

Then suddenly one day Harry said that he felt funny,
And everybody said, " Where Harry?" and he said,
"In the tummy,
It's mumbling and grumbling and it's heavy as a brick,
Be careful everyone, I think I'm going to be sick!"

And then Harry went,
"Bbbbbbllllliiiiirrrrgggggghhhhhhh!!"

And there it was, the biggest mess,
That anyone had ever seen,
And everybody looked at Harry,
Because Harry had gone green,
And said, "We don't want to be horrible,
And we don't want to be rude,
But you've only been that sick Harry,
Because you've eaten all that food."

Then from that day Harry decided,
It was better for his health,
If he ate the same amount of food,
As everybody else,
"And it's because" he told his mum, his dad, his teacher and his friends,
"I never ever want to be as sick as that again!"

Cheesy Charlie!

Charlie, just like everyone,
Really liked to eat,
He ate everything from crisps to fruit,
From cereal to meat,
When asked, "Would you like some food?"
Charlie always said, "Yes please",
And then he'd turn around and add,
"Oh yes, and could I have some cheese!"

For Charlie he just loved cheese,
All sorts of different kinds,
And it always seemed as if Charlie,
Just had cheese upon his mind,
And it wasn't just pure cheese he loved,
For he also liked to savour,
Any kind of any food,
That had a cheesy flavour.

And Charlie used to say,
"You know I think that life,
Would not be very easy,
If one day I could not get my hands,
On something nice and cheesy!"

Charlie ate cheese sandwiches,
And liked cheese sauce on chips,

He ate all sorts of cheesy crisps,
With all sorts of cheesy dips,
He would have cheese on his pasta,
And cheese upon his toast,
And cheese with any breakfast,
And even cheese with Sunday roast!

He would eat cheese in his bedroom,
And in the corridor at school,
He would eat cheese on the playground,
And at the swimming pool,
He would eat cheese in the bathroom,
He would eat cheese in the street,
You know Charlie didn't even seem to mind,
The smell of cheesy feet!

And he always used to say,
"You know I think that life,
Would not be very easy,
If one day I could not get my hands,
On something nice and cheesy!"

Charlie would hide cheese in his pockets,
And stash cheese in his draws,
And tuck cheese in his trousers,
He had all kinds of 'cheesy stores',
He would chomp cheese in the garden,
And chew cheese in the shed,
He would even nibble bits of cheese,

Whilst tucked away in bed!

Charlie would eat cheese in the daylight,
And even after dark,
He would take cheese to his friend's house,
And take cheese to the park,
In fact anything that Charlie did,
And anywhere he went,
Could always be associated,
With a cheesy scent.

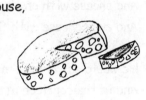

And Charlie would always say,
"You know I think that life,
Would not be very easy,
If one day I could not get my hands,
On something nice and cheesy!"

But then it was in his bed one day,
Whilst young Charlie was asleep,
That a nightmare about cheese,
Into his head did creep,
And Charlie dreamt that just because,
He'd eaten so much cheesy stuff,
That cheese itself wanted revenge.
For the cheese had had enough.

For in his dream Charlie dreamt,
That he was being chased,
By a massive cheesy monster,

With a nasty cheesy face,
And then they had a cheesy fight,
In which Charlie he got beaten,
And because he lost the fight,
Young Charlie then got eaten!

Then Charlie woke up in a sweat,
And realised it wasn't true,
And with one big sigh of relief,
Charlie just went, "Ppheww!"
Then in the morning whilst at breakfast,
Charlie wasn't even able,
To take a look at the chunk of cheese,
Placed upon the table.

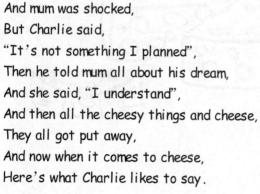

And mum was shocked,
But Charlie said,
"It's not something I planned",
Then he told mum all about his dream,
And she said, "I understand",
And then all the cheesy things and cheese,
They all got put away,
And now when it comes to cheese,
Here's what Charlie likes to say.

"I used to love my cheese you know,
And all that cheesy stuff,
When it came to eating cheese,
I just could not get enough.

But now I think that life,
Would not be very easy,
If I always had to eat,
Any food that's just all cheesy!"

Johnny 'Wriggler' Roberts!

Little Johnny Roberts,
A nickname he did earn,
'Wriggler' they called him,
For he wriggled like a worm!

Rarely would young Johnny,
Ever keep himself still,
He just wriggled and wriggled and wriggled,
Of his own free will!

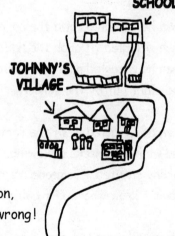

And people said to Johnny,
"If you keep wriggling away,
You'll wriggle into trouble
One fine day!"

But Johnny never listened,
He just kept wriggling on,
But he should have paid attention,
For those people they weren't wrong!

For one bright and breezy morning,
Whilst in his class at school,
Something happened to young Johnny,
That he did not expect at all.

He felt like being naughty,
So to make his classmates giggle,
He sat down on the carpet,
And just began to wriggle!

He started with his toes,
Going from the bottom to the top,
But when his teacher called out, "That's enough",
Johnny found he couldn't stop!

And then his wriggling took him out of the classroom!

Then he wriggled down the corridor,
Then wriggled through the hall,
Then he wriggled past the office,
And right out of the school!

Then he wriggled down the footpath,
And with his cheeks a blowing,
Johnny shouted, "Someone help me,
I don't know where I'm going!"

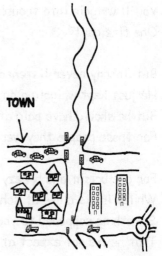

And people tried to stop him,
But it just wasn't to be,
For every time somebody caught him,
Johnny wriggled free!

And so he wriggled out of the village,
Past the pub, 'The Golden Crown',

Down the long and winding lanes,
And all the way to town!

Where he called out loud and clear once more,
"Help me please do,
If I don't stop wriggling soon,
Who knows where I'll wriggle to!"

And so more people came to help him,
Some were young and some were old,
But it really wasn't any good,
For no one could grab a hold!

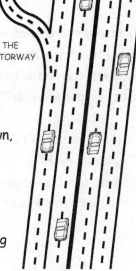

THE
MOTORWAY

So without the help he wriggled on,
And by the end of the day,
He'd gone right through and out of town,
And reached the motorway!

And Johnny thought within his head,
My wriggling now is just no fun,
I never dreamt this morning's wriggling
Would make me reach the M1!

And so he wriggled up to Milton Keynes,
On past Leicester and Nottingham,
And before long he'd wriggled 200 miles,
From where his wriggling began!

And in the order of the news,
Johnny's story it was top,
And all the headlines read,
'Just where will he stop'?

But he wriggled on past fields,
And over rivers full of reeds,
And by early the next morning,
He'd made the outskirts of Leeds!

By now he had crowds watching,
They lined the streets to view,
And everyone was asking,
"Just what can we do?"

So then everybody told him,
"Try as we might,
We just can't stop you wriggling,
For we just can't hold on tight!"

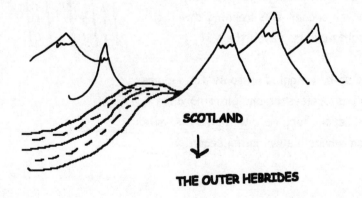

SCOTLAND

THE OUTER HEBRIDES

Some were trying to be helpful,
As some snacks they were throwing,
But Johnny thought, 'my word
Perhaps the food just keeps me going'!

So he stopped eating!
But alas it made no difference!

And so Johnny he just wriggled,
On his back, front, hands and knees,
Through the valley's up in Scotland,
Towards the Outer Hebrides!

And the whole country watched the news,
For they all wanted to see,
Just what would happen to young Johnny,
As he wriggled towards the sea!

But as he touched the water,
Little Johnny he just flopped,
For miracle of miracles,
All his wriggling just stopped!

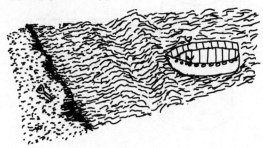

And so everybody realised ...

That if you want to stop some wriggling,
In order to succeed,
Quite simply some water,
Is all that you will need!

And Johnny announced on TV.

"From this day whenever I'm to sit upon the floor,
Never shall I make attempts to wriggle anymore!"

So to all you little wrigglers,
Be sure to understand,
That if you keep on wriggling,
Keep some water close at hand,
For if you don't then your wriggling,
May not go quite as planned,
And you may one day find yourself,
Wriggling right across the land!

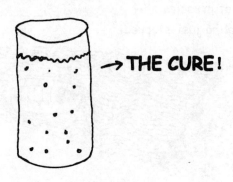

→ **THE CURE!**

The Staff Room

There's a secret room in every school,
Where teachers chill out and act cool!
It's full of biscuits and treats galore,
And it says 'Staff Room' on the door.

For only teachers are allowed in there,
You can't go in, you shouldn't dare!
Except of course if you're asked to go,
And then of course as you all know,
Dear children it is just a sin,
If you do not knock before you go in!

For behind that door the teachers (the staff),
All dance about and sing and laugh,
And in order to let go of their worries and cares,
They jump up and down on the tables and chairs!
And nibble the biscuits to fill their 'tums',
And at each other flick the crumbs!

They often like to paint their faces,
And round the room they run some races,
And have competitions to see who can,
Stay up the longest in a handstand!
Then to help them relieve their stress,
They all dress up in fancy dress,
So the 'Staff Room' at lunch is full of all sorts of things,

From witches, to fairies, from cowboys to kings!

And sometimes they go skipping,
Or just play with their toys,
And generally they make loads of noise,
In fact dear children, believe me it's true,
Those teachers they act just like you,
And that's why you must knock before in you go,
For those teachers they don't want you to know!
As when you knock it warns them all,
To sit down and look sensible!

Yes ...

There's a secret room in every school,
Where teachers go to break the rules.
So the 'Staff Room' those teachers do adore,
For they can all crazy behind that door!

The Head!

Classroom noisy,
Lots of screaming,
Loads of laughing,
Smiles beaming,
Using rulers,
As 'springy' tools,
To flick about,
Small paper balls.

But oh no, look out,
Here comes the head,
So suddenly,
Silence instead,
One whole room,
Filled with dread,
What's someone done?
What's someone said?

But ... phew,
He's gone!

Corridor messy,
Coats in a bunch,
Where's my coat?
It's time for lunch,
So much stuff,

Took a tumble,
All coats and me,
Then one BIG BUNDLE!

But oh no, look out,
Here comes the head,
So suddenly,
We're still instead,
Everybody's face is red,
With shoulders forward,
And hanging head.

But ... phew,
He's gone!

Playground busy,
Scores are level,
Till goal is scored,
By little Neville,
They score one back,
This game is tight,
Then one bad tackle,
One big fight!

But oh no, look out,
Here comes the head,
He pulls out Neville,
He pulls out Ted,
Can't look at him,

Just stare ahead,
Then, "You young man",
The voice it said.

OH NO!

Office quiet,
Don't deserve this,
Everybody,
Feeling nervous,
Anxious faces,
Sit and wait,
No one certain,
Of their fate.

And oh no, look out,
Here comes the head,
Those legs,
They must be made of lead,
Such a heavy,
Pounding tread,
And here he is,
Oh no, we're dead!!

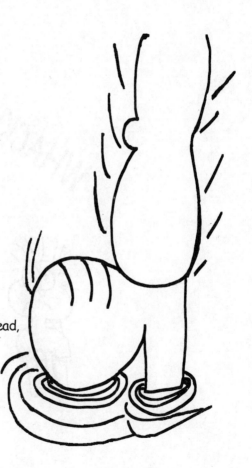

Bottom sore,
Rest of the day,
Feeling low,
Not much to say,
Just want to go home,

Away from the head,
Just want to go home,
Straight to bed!

Teachers

Oh those teachers, those teachers,
What are they about?
They talk a lot,
And sometimes they shout!

They're hard to work out,
As they're full of surprises,
And they come in all sorts,
Of shapes and sizes!

They make me read books,
And give me work,
Sometimes those teachers,
Drive me berserk!

But overall,
Those teachers,
They're nice,
For I'd never learn much,
Without their advice.

So all in all,
It's plain to see,
Without those teachers,
I just wouldn't be me!

Supply Teachers

Now they come to teach in your classroom,
Usually for a day or two,
And they're made out of plastic, elastic and paper,
Sellotape, sticks and glue!

For they're not a real teacher oh no!
Not like the ones you adore,
For when they turn up in the morning,
They come fresh from a factory floor!

Where they're made and upgraded or just simply tweaked,
Then programmed with school work and rules,
Then packed into boxes, stacked onto trucks,
And delivered fresh to all the schools!

And in the world of 'supply' here's how it's done,
When a real teacher's away your school orders one,
It's delivered real early so you don't get to see,
Your head teacher unpack it and set it free!

Then when you see them they look real 'life-like',
For they breathe, they laugh and they cough,
But please be aware; you must treat them with care,
For if you don't all their bits may fall off!

So if they're just a bit stiff and a little bit cranky,
You'll just need to give them some oil,
And don't worry if you hear any creaking or rattling,
It's just their nuts, bolts, springs and coils!

Yes to get the best out of supply teachers,
You must treat them with respect,
Just follow these rules as best you can,
So they don't fall into neglect.

Don't leave them out in the sun too long,
Don't stick them out in the rain,
For their microchips will just frazzle,
Or they'll end up with a rusty brain!

And don't be too noisy, naughty or cheeky,
Or they'll go into overload,
And steam will come whistling out of their ears,
And their head will just explode!

So treat your manufactured supply teacher well,
For you will find; that way,
They won't breakdown or completely malfunction,
They'll just give you a wonderful day!

A Day's Supply Teaching
(In a New Class from a Male Perspective)!

One or two scruffy ones,
Who love to mess about,
Three or four who think that when you talk,
You have to shout!

One or two who sit there,
Too shy to say a word,
Three or four who just look blank,
For all you've said they haven't heard!

One or two who always feel,
That to the toilet they must go!
Three or four who think it's necessary,
To tell you everything they know.

One or two who can't keep still,
And have to fiddle with all their stuff!
Three or four who before you've even started,
Look like they've had enough!

One or two 'bruiser' types,
Who act all big and bold,
And only three or four who work hard,
And just do as they are told!

Then the whole class,
Who altogether seem to just insist,
That although you are a Mr,
They have to call you Miss !

And all of this to work with,
When to work is just your aim,
Yet no work or plan is left behind,
And you don't know a single name !

And so 'Oh my world please help me',
In your head you cry,
When starting with a new class,
On a day's supply !

MR ->

MISS ->

I Don't Like My Classroom

I don't like my classroom,
It's smelly and old,
In the summer it's hot,
And in winter it's cold,
There are not enough windows,
And it's too near the hall,
And when my class are all in it,
It's just far too small.

I don't like my classroom,
It's too dark and too dim,
When I'm out in the playground,
I don't want to come in,
There's not enough colour,
And not enough space,
And not enough carpet,
It's just not a nice place!

I don't like my classroom,
It's just not for me,
It's nothing compared to the classrooms of year three!
We've too many 'bits' in it,
And far too much 'stuff',
When it comes to my classroom,
I've just had enough!

I don't like my classroom,
It always seems dusty,
And after the holidays,
It always smells musty,
There are not enough cupboards,
And not enough shelves,
You know I don't even think,
The children like it themselves!

I Hate Homework

I hate homework,
It makes me feel sick,
If I could choose what to do after school,
It's something I'd never pick,
I wish I were Head Teacher,
For then I'd make a rule,
That stated 'No one ever again is to do work outside of school'!

I hate homework,
It really is a bore,
If I could choose what to do after school,
I wouldn't choose homework for sure,
I wish I were the Teacher,
For then I would just say,
"I've had enough of giving out homework,
So just go home and play!"

I hate homework,
I always struggle through it,
If I could choose what to do after school,
You know I'd never choose to do it,
I wish I were my parents,
For then I'd write a letter that read,
Our child is allergic to homework,
It gives them an ache in the head!

I hate homework,
It really is no fun,
If I could choose what to do after school,
I'd choose that it never gets done,
I wish I were all that I've thought of,
But I'm not; so it is just my fate,
That I've no choice at all,
About what to do after school,
So I'm stuck with the homework I hate!

YUKKY HOMEWORK!

Food Dreams!

It's nearly lunchtime,
I'm having food dreams,
Oh please let it be nuggets,
With chips and with beans.

Or maybe today,
The special main course,
Is Bolognese,
With loads of sauce.

I'm feeling so hungry,
I just cannot wait,
It might roast chicken,
That appears on my plate.

With roast potatoes and yorkshires,
Oh what a treat,
When's that bell going?
I just want to eat!

And what of dessert,
Oh my dreams just can't stop,
It may be ice cream,
With chocolate on top!

Or maybe it's custard,
All dribbled on cake,
Oh come on,
It must be time for lunch break.

And it is!!!
I'm in the hall now,
I'm down on my knees,
Is it one of my dreams?
Oh please let it be, please.

Here is my plate,
And here is my bowl,
It's ... fish, peas and rice pudding,
And it' s all gone cold!

I Adoor Spelin!

I luv spelin tess,
I kan spel werds a plente,
Sow evre tymm I du wun,
I get twente owt ov twente!

Thhancuu faw reedin thiss pooim!

The Photographer's In

The photographer's in,
He's come to take shots,
Of mouths full of braces and faces with spots,
Of hair that's all greasy and slicked to one side,
Or shaven, or platted, or coloured or dyed!

Of crumpled up uniforms all covered in dust,
And blazers and ties that are all the wrong size!
Of shoes all scuffed up and knee high socks,
And torn trousers, skirts, blouses, shirts, dresses and frocks.

Of big cheeky grins or serious faces,
Or fidgety folk and gormless gazes!
Of wide eyes, or big ears, or thin lips, or large noses,
Of 'slouchers' or posers with posh little poses!

Of tired expressions or frustrated stares,
Of looks full of boredom or just simply mean glares!
Yes the photographer's in to spend his day,
With all those great people, just snapping away!

And what's wonderful is, that when his work's done,
The photographs will be loved, each and every one,
For they'll rest in an album or be placed on the side,
And for years shall be looked at with love and with pride.

Who is Alien?

Out there in Space; among all the stars,
Living on planets like Pluto and Mars,
Could be hundreds and thousands of horrible creatures,
Of all different sizes with gross ugly features!

Some with no heads and eyes in their arms,
Some covered in slime with teeth on their palms,
Others just blobs with inexplicable looks,
Or hundreds of tentacles shaped liked hooks.

Now an extra terrestrial I would like to see,
For this is how man thinks they would be,
Nothing but things of a hideous form,
Although they might not be far off the norm!

They might live in a house and have to pay bills,
And travel in trains, planes and automobiles,
And have beautiful countries, big cities with lights,
And live like on earth, by days and by nights.

And maybe they'll look just like a man,
With one head, two legs, two arms, two hands,
And they might think and act and do like we do,
Yes maybe they're just like me or like you.

And I'm sure this means like us they ponder,
Look at their sky and stop and wonder,
What on earth can be out there apart from them?
And what does it look like and then ...

They start to imagine the worst thing they can,
Creatures with claws and eyes big as pans,
Long slimy tongues and thick scaly skin,
And they shudder to think and go cold within.

But what they don't know as they look out afar,
Is that what lives out there is just like they are,
And that brings up my point as I write with my pen,
I often do wonder, who is alien?

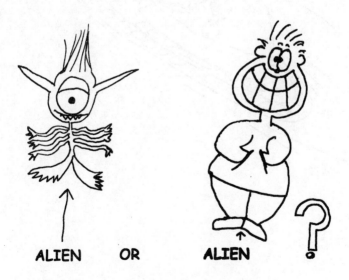

ALIEN   OR   ALIEN

UFO's

UFO's are mainly thought to be aliens from outer space,
Flying in and out our orbit whilst astray,
But if you mount up all the facts,
I cannot help but consider that,
Most are probably humans trying to get away!

Space

I have a great big spaceship,
A really funky machine,
It flies around at super speeds,
And is painted funky green,
I've entered a competition,
I've got to win the race,
The winner is the person,
Who flies around the whole of space!

Mixed Commentary

"She throws the ball up in the air, swipes the racquet",

"And yes it's there",

"A cracking goal for all to see",

"The crowd goes wild",

"What will it be?"

"It's a long one that's for sure",

"400 metres just one lap more",

"Here they come round the last bend",

"And",

"Oh he's off, that's surely the end",

"A tremendous spin by number four",

"And is she, yes she spins once more",

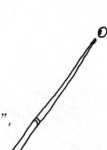

"Beautifully done as she comes to a halt",

"Now let's see what the judges thought",

"What a great score before being bowled out",

"A truly great player without a doubt",

"Yes, clears the table with such style",

"Shows no mercy as they hit the last mile",

"All bunched together towards the line",

"And he takes the yellow shirt for the first time",

"It takes a lot to get that fit",

"And oh my what a hit",

"He's out for the count, he can't go on",

"As they round the bend for the last furlong",

"It's Magic Moment in the lead",

"They cross the line, what a speed",

"Down the field look at him fly",
"All the way what a magnificent try",
"But will it be, oh my lord",
"He's done it, a new World Record!"

Ten Lines

Here is the first, the seconds to come,
And this being two means the last it was one,
This is the third, the one before four,
And now it's the fourth, or the third plus one more,
Now this fifth one out of the middle it sticks,
Sitting neatly between the fourth and this sixth,
And now we'll stick in the seventh before it's too late,
Which takes us to this, that is number eight,
And so close to the end here is number nine,
Which brings up the finish that is the tenth line!

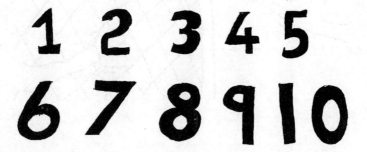

Poetry's Boring!

Poetry's boring,
Oh yes it is so,
If you've come to read poems,
I just don't want to know!

For it's trashy,
It's horrible,
It's silly and tiring!

It's dreary,
It's stupid,
And so uninspiring!

It's horrid,
It's gloomy,
It's yucky and ghastly.

It's uncool,
It's awful,
And seriously nasty!

Yes poetry's rubbish,
It really does stink,
It's dull and it's grey,
That's what I think.

But what's that you say?

Poetry's wicked,
It can make us all laugh,
It's funny and wacky,
It's crazy and daft.

It's great and it's good,
It's brilliant,
It's cool.

It's groovy,
It's neat,
And fantastic and all!

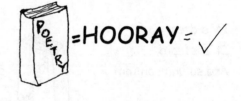 =HOORAY= ✓

It's loved,
It's popular,
And it entertains us.

It's adored by the world,
And it makes people famous.

Well if that's the case,
Then I tell you what,
I can't say poetry's boring,
For quite clearly it's not!

"Check Me Out!"

"Now check me out, I'm just so cool,
I'm just 'the bomb' I say,
I'm just so slick; I'm just so sly,
No-one's cooler than me no way!"

"Yes check me out, I'm just so smooth,
I'm fresh; I'm fly, it's true,
I'm just 'the business',
So check me out,
'Coz' I'm cooler than all of you!"

"Oh really!"

"Well hold up my friend; stop right there,
Just take a minute; just wait,
And ask yourself what makes you cool?"
"Yes just what makes you so great?"

"What makes you hip?"
"What makes you wicked?"
"Just what makes you the dude?"
"What have you done that's so 'off the hook',
And gives you right to this attitude?"
"In truth ... NOTHING!"

"So be careful my friend,
For all you've said is just so easy to say,
But if you've not proved it true to anyone,
Then you are not cool, no-way!"

Are you cool or not ?

The Singer

I shall sing, I shall sing,
Till all my days are done,
For I'm a singer,
And I'll refuse to die,
With any song unsung!

The Writer

I shall write, I shall write,
Until my body does decease,
For I'm a writer,
And I'll refuse to die,
With any unwritten piece!

The Fox

Bushy tail,
Eyes so bright,
Prowling round,
The streets at night,
When it's dark,
Up in the sky,
You see the fox,
All sneaky and sly.

The Owl

A wonderful site,
A creature of flight,
To be found in a barn,
Or some woods in the night.

Eyes burning bright,
Reflecting moonlight,
Spreading its wings,
It swoops like a kite.

Spotting its prey, from the treetops it soars,
Grabbing away with sharp extended claws.

I'd Rather Be a Cat

I'd rather be a cat,
Than anything else,
For if I could choose at my own free will,
I'd make a beeline,
To becoming a feline,
For all attention it would be mine,
When I wished of course!

And oh how hard my day would be,
Resting,
In the sun, or perhaps by the fire,
And 'turning up' when hungry,
After prowling round my territory.

You see,
What more could one need,
Than to gain so much affection,
With no effort in one's mannerisms,
Nothing I think,
So that is that,
I'm sure I'd rather be
a cat.

In a Tree!

Birds all sitting in a tree,
Use their wings to set them free,
And with all the things in the world to see,
I wonder why this can't be me!

Sweets!

Sugar,
Wears out all your teeth, so
Eat carefully for, as you might know,
Eating lots of sticky sweets means,
That one-day only your gums might
Show!

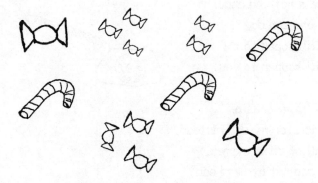

Who's On The Line?

I've just called my Nan,
She shouted, "Hello",
For who's on the line?
Is all she wants to know!

She calls out quite loudly,
For she's at the stage,
Where the hearing goes funny.
(They call it old age)!

There's nothing about it
That one can do,
It will happen to me,
It will happen to you.

And I'm my cousin,
My uncle, or my dad instead,
For all of those names
Just pop out of her head.

And she searches the names,
To find the right one
Until, "It's Neil" I say,
"Your lovely grandson!"

"I rang to say hi,
And have a quick chat,
To see if you're well,
And discuss this and that!"

Now I feel it's amusing,
And really quite endearing,
The mistakes we can make,
When we've trouble with our hearing.

For my aunt once went out,
Just to buy some Satsuma's,
And my Nan asked, "Why on earth,
Do you want some black bloomers?"

And I know that one-day,
Like my Nan I will be,
For grand-children they will smile,
When it's time to call me.

For I'll call out loud,
Shouting, "Hello",
For who's on the line?
Is all I'll want to know!

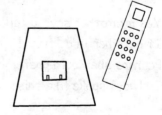

Speedy Speech!

(To be read out as quickly as possible)!

My mother says I talk too fast,
And says that people should,
Not talk as quickly as I do,
'Coz' it really isn't good!

She tells me, "Oh my word my boy,
Your speech is not so grand,
For when you speak; your speedy speech,
People just can't understand!

And she tells me, "My advice to you is,
Slow it down my dear,
For if you're always speaking 'speedy speech',
Your speech just isn't clear.

Yes my mother says I talk so fast,
It gets her in a 'tizz'!
Perhaps she would prefer it if ...
I always spoke like this!

(Last sentence to be read as slowly as possible)!

The Box!

"Think outside the box" they say,
"And that will make you cool",
But just why bother in the first place,
To get in 'the box' at all!

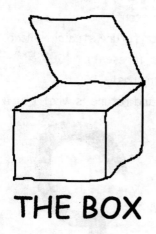

THE BOX

Where Am I ?

At present, I'm in the present,
But soon I'll be in the future,
Then the present I'm in now will be the past,
But once I reach the future,
It will become my present,
Then the past will be the present I was in last.

So now I'm in the future,
Or once again my present,
And there is another future straight ahead,
So soon this future, (present),
Will again become my past,
And a new present and future is what I'll have instead!

A Poet I Am!

So many words float in my head,
I write them down so they can be read,
For I love to write a line or two,
To be read by me or by you,
For you know I do prefer by choice,
To write rather than use my voice,
For my writing really sets me free,
And what do I write?
Well Poetry!

For I know what I am,
And I show what I am,
I write poems,
And so a poet I am!

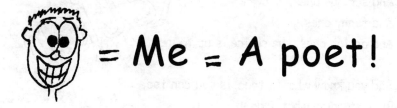 = Me = A poet!

A Poem About Poetry

Poetry, how great it is,
I write it all the time,
If they said "Line up to write poems",
I'd be the first in line.

For I love to write, both day and night,
Of that there is no doubt,
And I just can't stop my writing,
For there's so much to write about.

And all I do is write down,
What I think or feel,
About anything I choose,
Whether imaginary or real.

And I write short ones,
And long ones,
And serious ones,
And funny ones,
And action ones, the choice is up to me.

And you know what's true, is you can too,
By just doing what I do
For like that a poet you will be.

NOTHING

A Poem from Nothing

I'm trying to think of a poem,
But my brain will not allow,
Mind you I still write anyhow,
So although my mind is blank,
And I have an empty head,
My words can still be read,
And it seems I write a poem,
Without my knowing!

A Garden of Poems

There rests within my mind one thousand seeds,
That I shall drop on paper and grow for you to read,
For each poem that is within my power,
Is for me like one of nature's flowers,
For it starts so small and does transpire,
Into something that all can admire,
And such poems they are for me,
My beautiful garden for all to see.

For You To Read

I write these poems,
These poems I write,
Day after day,
Night after night.

And for you I hope,
I hope for you,
That you like more,
Than just one or two!

As nice it would be,
It would be nice,
If you read them all,
And more than twice!

For might you read,
Read you might,
Day after day,
Night after night.

And so I'll write more,
Yes indeed,
More I'll write,
For you to read!

Expression!

Show me ... delighted,
Show me ... excited,
Show me ... you're fully prepared.

Show me ... you're vicious,
Show me ... delicious,
Show me ... you're frightened and scared.

Show me ... big,
Show me ... bold,
Show me ... really cold,
Show me ... that you're concentrating.

Show me ... hungry for food,
Show me ... being rude,
Show me ... you're standing and waiting.

Show me ... you're thinking,
Show me ... you're winking,
Show me ... you're totally bored.

Show me ... be wary,
Show me ... be scary,
Show me ... that goal you just scored.

Show me ... I'm strong,
Show me ... what's wrong?
Show me ... you're feeling alone.

Show me ... you're sad,
Show me ... you're bad,
Show me ... I'm on the phone.

Show me ... having fun,
Show me ... on the run,
Show me ... I'm seriously hot.

Show me ... I'm great,
Show me ... just wait,
Show me quite simply ... what?

Show me ... hush hush,
Show me ... in a rush,
Show me ... stuck on the end of your nose.

Show me ... watching telly,
Show me ... phwoar, smelly,
Show me ... moving around on tiptoe.

Show me ... it's time to go,
Show me ... I don't really know,
Show me ... I've really been trying.

Show me ... tired and sleepy,
Show me ... down and quite weepy,
Show me ... you've really been crying.

Show me ... having a laugh,
Show me ... cleaning the bath,
Show me ... scrubbing and washing your face.

Show me ... I don't like that,
Show me ... take off that hat.
Show me ... you're all over the place.

Show me ... cleaning and dusting,
Show me ... that's disgusting,
Show me ... you're really tall.

Show me ... having a scoff,
Show me ... showing off,
Show me ... you're ever so small.

Show me ... you're really tough,
Show me ... I've had enough,
Show me ... so sweet and so nice.

Show me ... a shout,
Show me ... jumping about,
Show me ... hopping, not once but twice.

Now well done to you all,
That's the end of this lesson,
You really are all,
Masters of expression!

WELL

DONE!

Down in The Jungle

Down in the jungle,
Strolling along,
What's that noise?
Something's wrong.

LOOK!

Wrapped round a tree,
Nice and tight,
Is a big snake hissing,
And it's looking for a bite.

We'll have to move faster!

Down in the jungle,
Walking along,
What's that noise?
Something's wrong.

LOOK!

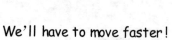

Coming out of the river,
With a scaly back,
Is a crocodile snapping,
And it's looking for a snack.

We'll have to move faster!

Down in the jungle,
Marching along,
What's that noise?
Something's wrong.

LOOK!

Thumping its chest,
With all its might,
Is a grumpy gorilla,
And it's looking for a fight.

We'll have to move faster!

Down in the jungle,
Running along,
What's that noise?
Something's wrong.

LOOK!

Over in the bushes,
Sitting on a hump,
Is a big lion roaring,
And it's ready to jump.

We'll have to move faster!

Down in the jungle,
Sprinting along,
What's that noise?
Something's wrong.

LOOK!

It's a big herd of elephants,
All of them grey,
They're not very happy,
And they're stomping our way!

We'll have to move faster!

Down in the jungle,
Charging along,
But STOP, wait a minute,
The noise is all gone!

No snakes hissing,
No crocodiles snapping,
No gorillas thumping,
No lions roaring,
No elephants stomping!

HOORAY, we're safe!

Me, I Love To Play a Drum

Me, I love to play a drum,
I love to hit a beat,
And whilst I play all I ask,
Is that you all move your feet.

For I have a little rhythm,
In the corner of my mind,
So I'll play it and you move,
And be sure to keep in time.

(Play drum).

Me, I love to play a drum,
Of that there is no doubt,
And whilst I play all I ask,
Is that you all dance about.

I'll play a little quicker now,
And I'll watch to see,
If anyone around the room,
Can dance so gracefully.

(Play drum).

Me, I love to play a drum,
For good rhythms are a gift,

And whilst I play, all I ask,
Is that you make your bodies shift.

I'll play it even quicker now,
And whilst you're in the groove,
I'll keep an eye upon you,
To see how well you all can move.

(Play drum).

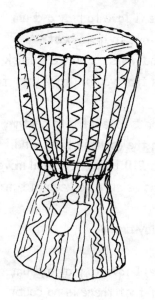

Me, I love to play a drum,
Yes, sweet drumming is my thing,
And whilst I play, all I ask is,
That you get into the swing.

I'll play it even quicker now,
So get ready here we go,
It's time for us to put on,
One great big dancing show!

(Play drum).

Me, I love to play a drum,
So all sit down and that's what I'll do,
For now I'll play the drum as best I can,
Just for all of you!

(Play drum).

Don't Hang Around!

Now I'll tell you a story of some men in a boat,
Who away to an island one day did float,
They landed on the shore and explored through the trees,
And whilst they explored they heard drums like these!

At the sound of the drums they stood still one and all,
Then one of the men said, "You know I recall,
That drums in the jungle are a dangerous sign,
And listen everyone they're getting louder all the time!"

So the men ventured on trying to get away,
But deeper and deeper they did stray!
They were thirsty; they were weary from the jungle heat,
And louder and louder grew the beat!

Then there through a clearing the men did spy,
Fires burning and smoke in the sky,
And people all chanting and dancing in a crowd,
And banging their drums, which were now this loud!

And they chanted ...

"We are the jungle people and we dance to our beat,
And all kinds of things we love to eat,
Boil it; roast it, put it in a stew,
And if we ever find you then we'll gobble up you!"

And then they saw the men!

And as the men turned away they heard the people say ...

"We are the jungle people and we dance to our beat,
We've seen those men, who we'd love to eat,
Boil them; roast them, put them in a stew,
Run like mad because we're coming for you!"

But the men they ran; fast across the ground,
And with a bit of luck their boat they found,
Pushed off; jumped in and rowed away,
And the sound of the drums slowly faded away.

Now the moral of my story I must say,
Is if you're lost in the jungle one fine day,
And you stumble through the trees and hear this sound,
Then my friends don't hang around!

Let's Go Down To The Beach

Let's go down to the beach,
Where underneath the sun,
We'll spend all day playing away,
And having loads of fun.

Don't forget your bucket,
And don't forget your spade,
You can't go without them,
For there's sandcastles to be made.

Let's walk along the seafront,
Let's run along the sand,
Let's explore the rock pools,
Let's pick up shells by hand.

Let's chase the waves as they flow out,
Then wait and watch, and then ...
Turn and run away,
When they flow back in again.

Let's jump into the water,
And swim so you don't get chilly,
Let's wave our arms all about,
And splash each other silly.

Let's play football with a beach ball,
And when the wind, it blows,
Let's chase the ball down the beach,
As quickly off it goes.

Let's buy a great big ice cream,
And eat away without a care,
Then let's stop a while, sit down and relax,
In a great big springy deck chair.

Yes ...
Let's go down to the beach,
Where underneath the sun,
We'll spend all day playing away,
And having loads of fun.

The Jolly People's Boat Trip!

There were once some jolly people,
Who jumped aboard a boat,
And sailed it out to sea,
To see how well they all could float!

But the waves were a little high,
And the wind was a little bit strong,
And so as everybody sailed away,
It wasn't very long.

Before ...

They went left and right,
And were rocking all about,
And were hanging on quite tightly,
In case they all fell out!

Yes ...

There were once some jolly people,
Who jumped aboard a boat,
And sailed it out to sea,
To see how well they all could float!

But the waves got even higher,
And the wind became so strong,

119

And so as everybody sailed away,
It wasn't very long.

Before ...

They went up and down,
And were rocking all about,
And were hanging on so tightly,
In case they all fell out!

Yes ...

There were once some jolly people,
Who jumped aboard a boat,
And sailed it out to sea,
To see how well they all could float!

But the waves got even higher!
And the wind became really strong!
And so as everybody sailed away,
It wasn't very long

Before ...

They went this way and that way,
And were rocking all about,
And were hanging on really tightly,
In case they all fell out!

Yes ...

There were once some jolly people,
Who jumped aboard a boat,
And sailed it out to sea,
To see how well they all could float!

But the waves got ridiculously high,
And the wind got incredibly strong,
And so as everybody sailed away,
It wasn't very long.

Before ...

They went left and right and up and down,
This way and that way and were rocking all around!
And they hung on tighter than ever before whilst rolling all
about,
But in the end it wasn't any good for everyone fell out!

With a SPLISH and a SPLOSH,
And big SPLASHES galore,
And then those jolly old people all soaking wet,
All swam back to shore!

All Sorts of Noises
(The Onomatopoeia Poem)!

Down on the busy and noisy farm,
When out in the fields all the cows go ... "MOO!"

Up on the hill in the damp, dark, dreary;
Haunted house; all the ghosts go ... "BOO!"

There in your house when visitors come,
They push the doorbell and it goes ... DING DONG!

And high in the clock tower right at the top;
When the clock strikes 12 the bell goes ... BONG!

Now when you eat breakfast and you have a boiled egg,
You hit it with a spoon and the shell goes ... CRACK!

Out on the court when a tennis player serves;
The ball goes in the air and they give it a ... WHACK!

Down on the hot and crazy racetrack,
All of the cars they go with a ... ZOOM!

And back in the old days great big ships,
When they went into battle their cannons went ... BOOM!

If you go swimming and you jump in the pool,
You'll always hit the water with a great big ... SPLASH!

When you play football if you're not very careful,
You might hit a window and the glass will go ... SMASH!

If you take a really posh, fine glass,
Carefully flick it and you'll hear a ... TING!

And if you buy a shirt that's just too small
Try to do up the buttons and they'll all go ... PING!

Now if you have a bag and it's way too heavy,
When it drops to the floor it makes a big ... THUMP!

In the middle of the night when it's quiet and dark,
People are afraid of things that go ... BUMP!

Or out in woods in the middle of the night,
High up in the trees all the owls ... TWEET-TWOO!

And if you went out there you'd catch a cold,
And so all of the time you'd be going ... AAA-CHOO!

So it's ...

MOO!
BOO!

DING DONG!
BONG!

CRACK!
WHACK!

ZOOM!
BOOM!

SPLASH!
SMASH!

TING!
PING!

THUMP!
BUMP!

TWEET-TWOO!
AAA-CHOO!

And that's that!

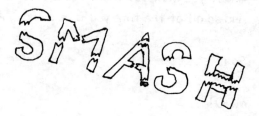

Now that's the end of this book,
So thanks dear friend for taking a look,
I hope you enjoyed every line,
And that you'll read it again some other time!